PREACHING PHILIPPIANS

Talk outlines for Paul's letter to the Philippians

CONTENTS

A. QUICK HELP: How to prepare a talk on Philippians . . . 4

B. How to use Preaching Philippians 5

C. About Paul's letter to the Philippians 7

D. Study and Preach Paul's letter to the Philippians 9

E. Lessons from Philippians 51

F. Training guide 53

Please read this first!

It is a big joy to bring you another PPP book. We pray that this will help you to preach God's word. We want people everywhere to hear God's word clearly. Then people will turn to Jesus. Christians will grow more like Jesus. God will have all the praise.

We give you a lot of help. But you must still work hard! Please do not just copy what you read!

PPP means Pray! Prepare! Preach! There is a lot to do before you preach.

PRAY. The best talk in the world is no good without God. Pray that you will speak God's truth. Pray that God will speak to people's hearts. Pray for yourself as you prepare. Pray that God's word will come alive to you.

PREPARE. You need several hours to prepare a Bible talk. Work hard to understand the Bible section. Think about the help that we have given you. Which parts will help your listeners? How can you explain it better? We only give you a few words. You need to say more, so that everyone understands.

PREACH. Now you can preach. It is a big joy when we know that we teach God's words. These are not things that we want to say. These are God's truths, written in his word. God has promised that they will do his work!
Isaiah 55:10-11

Here is the best way to use this book. Start at the beginning of Philippians and teach each section in turn. It is a letter. It makes most sense when you read it from the beginning.

'And my God will meet all your needs according to his glorious riches in Christ Jesus.' Philippians 4:19

At the back of this book there is more help for you on how prepare and give a talk.

Phil Crowter

A: QUICK HELP:
How to prepare a talk on Philippians

1. Pray for God's help.

2. 📖 Read the Bible section several times.
Use ▣ **Background** to help you to understand the section.
Use ▣ **Notes** to help you to understand difficult Bible verses.

3. Try to find the main point that God is teaching us in the Bible section.
Use ▣ **Main point** to help you.

4. Pray for your people. Think how this Bible section will help them.
Use ✶ **Something to work on** to help you

5. Write your talk in your own language. Start with the main points which the Bible teaches.
Use our notes in the **PREACH** section to help you.

6. Now write a beginning and an end for your talk.

7. Check what you have done.
- Is the **main point** clear?
- Do you show them what the **Bible** teaches?
- Do you use **word pictures** to help your people understand and remember?
- Do you **connect** with the people?
- What do you hope will **change**?

8. Pray that God will speak through your words. Pray that his truth will change people.

For more help read the next section.

B: How to use Preaching Philippians

Every time you prepare a talk, begin with these things:

- Pray for God's help

- Read the Bible section

- Try to find the main point that God is teaching us in the Bible section.

Then you can use these notes to help you. There are two pages for each talk. The first page helps you to think about the Bible section. The second page gives you headings and ideas for a talk.

When you see this symbol 📖 , you need to read what the Bible says.

STUDY PAGE: UNDERSTAND THE BIBLE

The first page helps you to understand the Bible section.

⬛ Background

It is important to think about what comes before and after the section. We will look at a few verses each time. However, those verses fit into Paul's whole letter to the Christians at Philippi. Always ask how a section carries on what Paul is saying.

The **Background** section will help you to do this.

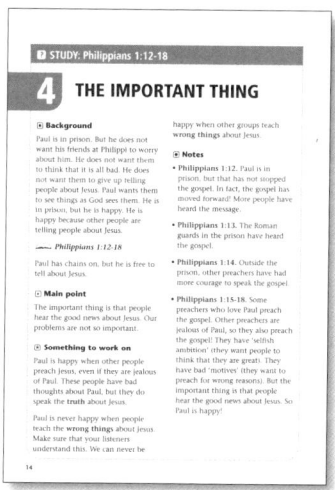

⬛ Main point

We have put the most important point in a few words. Think about this point. Can you see this is what the Bible section is teaching? Try to make sure that this point is very clear in your talk.

✴ Something to work on:

This section chooses something from the Bible section which you need to think about. It is important to work hard to understand the Bible. Think carefully about how to teach the point in this section.

⬛ Notes

This section tells you about difficult Bible verses. It will help you not to make mistakes when you teach.

PREACH PAGE:
TEACH THE BIBLE

The second page helps you to teach the Bible section. You must also do your own work. This page gives you ideas. You must take the ideas and use them in the best way. We give you the bones, but you must put the meat on the bones!

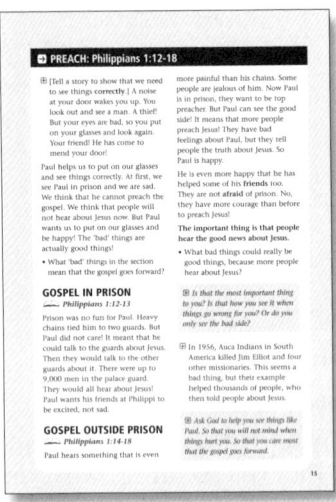

1. THINGS WE HAVE WRITTEN TO HELP YOU

- **Two or three headings.**

   These are written **LIKE THIS**. These headings will help you to teach the Bible clearly. You can change the headings to make them better for your people.

- **We show you what the Bible says.** We want people to listen to the Bible. Keep reminding them of what the Bible says. If they have a Bible, ask them to find the verse you are talking about. This symbol will help you know when to do this.

- **We explain what the Bible is teaching.** You need to think how to explain the Bible so that your people understand. You know your people. We do not know your people. Your words are better than our words.

- **We sometimes use a word picture.** Here is an example from the notes on Philippians 1:1-5.

   ⊕ *Men with a lorry came to take away some of my rubbish. We should be partners, as we all want to keep the streets clean. There were 15 bits of wood to collect. But the lazy men with the lorry only took 3 bits.*

   The word picture may not be good for your people. Perhaps you do not have lorries to collect rubbish. A Bible teacher must find a better word picture to help the people understand. You will need to find many more word pictures to help teach the Bible truth. Be very careful that the word picture teaches what the Bible is saying.

- **We show you how to connect the Bible teaching to your people.** It is important to hear God's word speaking **to us.** We need to know how the Bible teaching changes us. Here is an example:

   We give you one or two ideas. You need to think of more ways to connect the Bible to your people. You know the people. You know how the Bible needs to change their lives.

> To be partners we all need to serve. Do you serve other people?

2. OTHER THINGS YOU WILL NEED TO DO:

- **Think how to start your talk.** Your people need to see why it is important to listen today. Tell them what you will teach them from the Bible. Tell them why it is important for them.

- **Think how to end your talk.** Remind them of the main points. Give them something to think about, or something to do.

- **Pray!** You are telling the people God's truth from God's word. Pray that God will use your words to speak to the people. Pray that God's truth will change people.

- **Always use your own language. Never** say things in English, if the people do not speak English well.

C: About Paul's letter to the Philippians
Gospel thinking

Philippi was the first city in Europe that Paul visited. Philippi is in Greece. In the Bible, the area is called Macedonia (a little way from the country called Macedonia today).

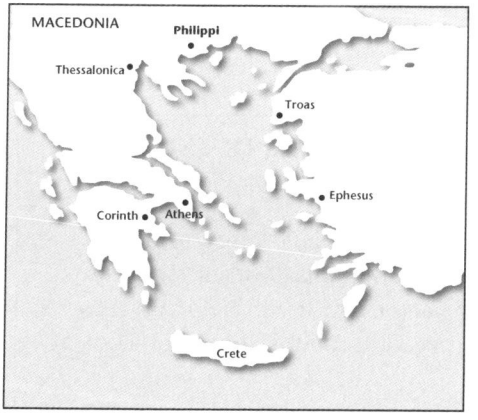

The believers at Philippi

📖 *Acts 16:6-40.* This was Paul's second missionary journey. The first people to become Christians in Philippi were Lydia and the prison guard. These people started the church at Philippi.

The church helped Paul in his missionary work. The Christians sent money, so that Paul did not have to work so much. This gave Paul great joy, because they loved the gospel as he did. They were his partners.

But there were three dangers in the church:
1. Some people hated the believers. They made life very difficult for them.

2. Some Jewish teachers taught wrong things. They said that you had to become a Jew to be a true Christian.
3. Sadly, some Christians thought wrongly about each other. There were quarrels.

Paul's letter

About 10 years after Paul first visited Philippi, he was in prison in Rome. (This was about 30 years after Jesus died, around 62 AD.) One day he had a visitor. It was Epaphroditus. He came all the way from Philippi (about 800 miles). Epaphroditus brought a gift from the church at Philippi.

Paul was so happy to see him! Epaphroditus was very sick on the journey. He took a long time to get better. When Epaphroditus was better, Paul wrote this letter to the church. Epaphroditus took it back to Paul's friends at Philippi. Here are some of the things that Paul says:

- Paul is so happy that they are still partners with him. He wants them to carry on telling people about Jesus.

- Paul warns them against the false teachers.

- Paul tells them to be humble, like Jesus. They must not quarrel.

In his letter, Paul helps them to **think right**. He gives them examples of people whose lives show that they think like Jesus. Everyone should copy these people! When we learn to think right, we will live right.

This letter has many important lessons for believers today. We work hard to understand what Paul said to them. Then we see how God's word speaks in a powerful way to us. This letter trains us to think in a way which puts Jesus and the gospel first. We need this so much in our lives and our churches!

At the back of the book you will find a section called **LESSONS FROM PHILIPPIANS**. You can use these questions after you have finished all the talks on Philippians. Or you may want to use them after each chapter.

At the back of this book you will also find a section called **TRAINING – how to preach Philippians**

This will help you, or even better, a group of preachers, to use this book. There are five studies to help you to preach Philippians yourself. This is so you do not have to depend as much on what we say. It will help you to work things out for yourself. It will train you to become a better preacher. Look at this **before** you use this book.

PREACHING PHILIPPIANS

D: Study and preach Paul's letter to the Philippians

STUDY: Philippians 1:1-5

PARTNERS IN THE GOSPEL

◉ Background

Paul is in prison in Rome. (Philippians 1:12-14). He cannot visit the Christians at Philippi. He cannot teach them about Jesus. But he can encourage these Christians. He can help them to keep going on.

Here is the first way Paul helps them. He shows how much they mean to him. Paul is an apostle. God has given him authority over the churches. But he writes as a 'servant' and friend who loves the Philippians. *Philippians 1:1-5.*

◉ Main point

Paul and the Philippian Christians are **partners**. They help each other in the work of the gospel.

(When Paul says 'gospel' he means the **whole** message about Jesus. The gospel of Jesus brings people to believe in Jesus, and it helps Christians to live for Jesus.)

⭐ Something to work on

Love for the same gospel glues Paul and the Philippian church together. What does this mean for us? How are we partners with other believers? (Example: we may give money to help missionaries.)

But it is not good to be partners with every church, or with everyone who says they are Christians. (At Philippi there were religious people who Paul wanted the Christians to stay away from; Philippians 3:2, 18-19.)

◉ Notes

- **Philippians 1:1.** 'Saints' ('God's people'). This means 'holy people'. Paul does not mean special Christians. He means every Christian. God calls us all to be holy (set apart for God).

- **Philippians 1:1.** 'Overseers.' There are different words for **church leaders** (overseer, bishop, pastor, elder). 'Deacons' ('helpers') help the church leaders.

- **Philippians 1:5.** 'Partnership in the gospel.' We talk about 'fellowship'. That word really means 'partnership'. God does not want Christians only to have a nice time together. He wants us to **work** together for the gospel. God wants to us help each other, to be partners.

➡ PREACH: Philippians 1:1-5

WHO ARE THE PARTNERS?
📖 *Philippians 1:1*

Paul and Timothy, SERVANTS

What an example to us all! The great apostle Paul calls himself a servant! Just like our great Saviour.

⊕ I heard of a church in Peru. Mostly poor people go there. Sometimes more educated people come. They have more money. And they think that they are important. They want to be **leaders**, **bosses**. How sad! If only they were willing to be **servants**, they could help so much.

» *To be partners we all need to serve. Do you serve other people?*

God's people in Philippi, SAINTS

Paul knows there are some problems in the church. But he still calls all the Christians 'saints'. This means 'holy people –set apart for God.' God has made Christians holy. He has washed us clean through the blood of Jesus.

» *Do you think of yourself as one of God's **holy** people? How will this show in your life?*

WHAT MAKES US PARTNERS?
📖 *Philippians 1:5*

What happens when you meet someone with the same interest? [Give examples.] You can talk for hours!

It is like that with the **gospel**. It is like glue that sticks us together with people who love the same message about Jesus. We feel really close to them. Then it is a joy to work with them, to be **partners**. We love to help them to tell people about Jesus. Is that how you feel? Think about this story:

⊕ Men with a lorry came to take away some of my rubbish. We should be partners, as we all want to keep the streets clean. There were 15 bits of wood to collect. But the lazy men with the lorry only took 3 bits.

» *Are you like those men? You say that you love the gospel, but you do not want to work very hard. Do you need to change? What can you do to play your part?*

So how can Paul and the Philippians work together as partners? Remember, Paul is in prison. He is a long way away! 📖 *Philippians 1:3-4* gives one way.

Prayer is a great way to help with the gospel. Look at Paul's joy as he thinks of his friends in Philippi! Think—who do you know who loves the gospel? Will you be a **partner**? Will you pray for them?

⬇ STUDY: Philippians 1:6-8

2 CONFIDENT

◉ Background

Paul and the Philippian Christians are **partners**. They help each other in the work of the gospel (Philippians 1:1-5). When you work together like this, you need to feel **confident** (sure) in each other. Now we see why Paul feels so happy about these believers.

Find the reasons in 📖 *Philippians 1:4-8*.

◉ Main point

Paul is very happy about these Christians. He can see **God** at work in their lives. And he can see **them** at work for the gospel.

✸ Something to work on

God's work and ours. God **always** works first. God saves us. God changes our hearts. And God makes sure that he finishes his work, so that none of his people is lost. (📖 *2 Timothy 1:12; John 10:27-28*.)

Our work—what **believers** do is because of what God has done in them. The Philippians worked with Paul in the gospel because God had worked in them to save them. (📖 *Philippians 2:13; Ephesians 2:10*.)

◉ Notes

- **Philippians 1:6.** 'Day of Christ Jesus.' This means the day when Jesus will come back. Then God's work in us will be finished.

- **Philippians 1:7.** 'Whether I am in chains or defending and confirming the gospel.' The Philippian Christians helped Paul in **prison** and in **preaching** about Jesus.

- **Philippians 1:7.** 'All of you share in God's grace with me' (NIV). Or, 'you have all shared with me in this privilege ('honour') that God has given me' (GNB). It is God's **gift** ('grace') to work for him. And it is a joy when other people share in the work.

- **Philippians 1:8.** God knows that it is true! Paul loves these Christians with deep feelings ('affection') that come from Jesus himself.

➡ PREACH: Philippians 1:6-8

'I am worried about him.' Have you ever thought that? Perhaps about a friend who said he trusted Jesus, but he does not seem to live like a Christian. Paul was **not** worried about the Christians at Philippi! He was confident about them. For two important reasons—

GOD'S WORK IN US
📖 *Philippians 1:6*

✚ Once, I started to make a model fire engine out of matchsticks. If I finished it would look nice. But it took too long. I got bored. I gave up.

• Praise God! He does not give up with us! What is Paul sure about?

Paul is not sure because these Christians are strong enough to carry on. He is not confident because they are very good Christians. He is confident in **God's work.** God never starts things and then gives up. God never calls people to belong to his family and then lets them go. God never looks at Christians and thinks that they will never finish. It may take a very long time, but God will always finish the work that he begins.

• If my fire engine had been very valuable, I would not have given up! Why does God not give up? (Ephesians 5:25-27)

» *We may feel that we are poor Christians. We disappoint Jesus so often. Perhaps we think that we will give up. Remember that God will not give up with us! We are far too valuable! Jesus has paid the price of his blood for us. And when Jesus comes, we will be perfect! God's work in us will be finished.*

OUR WORK FOR GOD
📖 *Philippians 1:7-8*

How was Paul so sure of God's work in these Christians? Partly because, in prison, he heard such good things about them. He heard how they were at work for the gospel. **Our work for God shows that God has worked in us.**

Remember **Philippians 1:5**. In Philippians 1:7, Paul says more about the way they shared with him in the gospel. Paul was in prison, so they cared for him. Someone travelled for weeks to bring Paul gifts in prison. Now that Paul could not carry on with the gospel work, they did it! See how full Paul is of joy and love for these Christians. He is confident about them!

» *Can other Christians be confident about you? Why or why not? How can you be more like these Philippian Christians?*

STUDY: Philippians 1:9-11

3 I PRAY FOR YOU

◉ Background

Paul is full of joy when he remembers these Christians. This is because he can see that God is at work in their lives. He is also happy because they are partners with him in the gospel work.

📖 *Philippians 1:3-8*

Paul wants these friends to **grow** as Christians. So he prays. Notice what he prays for. Think why he chooses these things.

📖 *Philippians 1:9-11*

◉ Main point

Paul prays for **more love**,

so that we **make the best choices**,

so that we **live for God's praise**.

⭑ Something to work on

Think how Paul's prayers can help our prayers. How do we pray for each other? How can you help your people to pray for the things here?

◉ Notes

- **Philippians 1:9.** Paul prays for two things here; more love and wise love. He wants them to love the right things.

- **Philippians 1:10.** When we love the right things, we will **choose** ('discern') the best things! When we choose the best things, we will **live** right lives ('pure and blameless').
  Then we will be ready for the day when Jesus comes.

- **Philippians 1:11.** When we choose the best things, we will have Jesus' **fruit** in our lives. He will produce good and holy things in us. That will bring glory and praise to God!

→ PREACH: Philippians 1:9-11

MORE, BETTER LOVE!
📖 *Philippians 1:9*

⊕ Imagine that you have a good, hot fire. You do not need to blow on it to make it hotter! You do not need to put any more wood on it!

The Philippian Christians already have warm love. Now it is as if Paul asks for more wood for the fire. He prays that their love may be even hotter!

And, not only hotter, but **wiser**. Even love can get out of control, like a fire. So Paul prays that they will know the right things to love.

- What are the right things to love? What about the wrong things? How can we tell?

If we read the Bible, we will grow to love the things that God loves.

> ⟫ *Does your Christian life sometimes get cold and lazy? Pray for more love! Pray for yourself and for other Christians. Pray that your love will be wise. Pray that you will love the things that God loves.*

BEST CHOICES
📖 *Philippians 1:10*

- What different choices do you make each day?

It does not matter what we choose to eat or wear. But it does matter what we choose to do, or say. And sometimes we have important decisions to make. Paul prays that we will know how to make the **best** choices.

God not only wants us to say no to bad things. Sometimes we need to say no to **good** things, so that we can choose the **best** things!

[Give some examples. Or, you could talk about this in groups. What are the best things to do, or to say? Then pray together that God will teach you to make the best choices.]

LIVE FOR GOD'S GLORY
📖 *Philippians 1:10-11*

When we make the best choices, what happens to our lives?

1. They do not have bad things in them (Philippians 1:10).

2. They have lots of good things in them (Philippians 1:11).

Then we will be ready for Jesus when he comes back. And our lives will bring praise and glory to God!

> ⟫ *Do you want **that** most of all? Not for **people** to think that you are good. You want **God** to get the praise! Pray Paul's prayer—God will say yes!*

STUDY: Philippians 1:12-18

4 THE IMPORTANT THING

◉ Background

Paul is in prison. But he does not want his friends at Philippi to worry about him. He does not want them to think that it is all bad. He does not want them to give up telling people about Jesus. Paul wants them to see things as God sees them. He is in prison, but he is happy. He is happy because other people are telling people about Jesus.

📖 Philippians 1:12-18

Paul has chains on, but he is free to tell about Jesus.

◉ Main point

The important thing is that people hear the good news about Jesus. Our problems are not so important.

✭ Something to work on

Paul is happy when other people preach Jesus, even if they are jealous of Paul. These people have bad thoughts about Paul, but they do speak the **truth** about Jesus.

Paul is never happy when people teach the **wrong things** about Jesus. Make sure that your listeners understand this. We can never be happy when other groups teach **wrong things** about Jesus.

◉ Notes

- **Philippians 1:12.** Paul is in prison, but that has not stopped the gospel. In fact, the gospel has moved forward! More people have heard the message.

- **Philippians 1:13.** The Roman guards in the prison have heard the gospel.

- **Philippians 1:14.** Outside the prison, other preachers have had more courage to speak the gospel.

- **Philippians 1:15-18.** Some preachers who love Paul preach the gospel. Other preachers are jealous of Paul, so they also preach the gospel! They have 'selfish ambition' (they want people to think that they are great). They have bad 'motives' (they want to preach for wrong reasons). But the important thing is that people hear the good news about Jesus. So Paul is happy!

➔ PREACH: Philippians 1:12-18

⊕ [Tell a story to show that we need to see things **correctly**.] A noise at your door wakes you up. You look out and see a man. A thief! But your eyes are bad, so you put on your glasses and look again. Your friend! He has come to mend your door!

Paul helps us to put on our glasses and see things correctly. At first, we see Paul in prison and we are sad. We think that he cannot preach the gospel. We think that people will not hear about Jesus now. But Paul wants us to put on our glasses and be happy! The 'bad' things are actually good things!

- What 'bad' things in the section mean that the gospel goes forward?

GOSPEL IN PRISON
📖 *Philippians 1:12-13*

Prison was no fun for Paul. Heavy chains tied him to two guards. But Paul did not care! It meant that he could talk to the guards about Jesus. Then they would talk to the other guards about it. There were up to 9,000 men in the palace guard. They would all hear about Jesus! Paul wants his friends at Philippi to be excited, not sad.

GOSPEL OUTSIDE PRISON
📖 *Philippians 1:14-18*

Paul hears something that is even more painful than his chains. Some people are jealous of him. Now Paul is in prison, they want to be top preacher. But Paul can see the good side! It means that more people preach Jesus! They have bad feelings about Paul, but they tell people the truth about Jesus. So Paul is happy.

He is even more happy that he has helped some of his **friends** too. They are not **afraid** of prison. No, they have more courage than before to preach Jesus!

The important thing is that people hear the good news about Jesus.

- What bad things could really be good things, because more people hear about Jesus?

❱❱ *Is that the most important thing to you? Is that how you see it when things go wrong for you? Or do you only see the bad side?*

⊕ In 1956, Auca Indians in South America killed Jim Elliot and four other missionaries. This seems a bad thing, but their example helped thousands of people, who then told people about Jesus.

❱❱ *Ask God to help you see things like Paul. So that you will not mind when things hurt you. So that you care most that the gospel goes forward.*

STUDY: Philippians 1:19-26

5 JESUS CHOICES

▣ Background

Paul has **prayed** that these Christians will make the best choices. 📖 *Philippians 1:9-11.* Now he gives his own example. Paul is in prison. He does not know what will happen to him. What would he choose?

Paul's choices are Jesus choices. 📖 *Philippians 1:19-26*

Paul does not want people to think that he is a wonderful Christian. He wants to show these believers how to think. God wants us to **think** right, so we **choose** right, so we **live** right. Paul wants his example to help us. 📖 *Philippians 3:17.*

▣ Main point

Paul longs to go to **be with** Christ. But it is even better to **serve** Christ.

▣ Something to work on

Paul cannot really choose whether he will live or die. He knows that is God's choice. But can you say that death is gain? Many people fear death. Help your listeners to see that, for believers, death is not something to fear. It takes them home!

▣ Notes

- **Philippians 1:19.** 'Deliverance' or 'set free' is the same word as '**salvation**'. Paul does not know what the Roman ruler (Caesar) will decide to do with him. But he does know that God will hear their prayers. Even if he dies, Paul is safe. Whatever happens, God will make it work for his 'salvation'. It will be good for Paul!

- **Philippians 1:20.** Even if Caesar kills him, Paul hopes for courage to honour Jesus.

- **Philippians 1:22-24.** Paul would love to go to be with Christ. But if he lives, there is gospel work to do. The Christians need him to help them.

- **Philippians 1:25-26.** So Paul believes that he will live. Paul wants to help them grow in their faith. He wants to give them joy when he sees them again.

➔ PREACH: Philippians 1:19-26

TO LIVE OR TO DIE?
📖 *Philippians 1:21-22*

❥ *Are you ready to live? Are you ready to die? Many people find life too hard – but death seems even worse! Why is Paul so different?*

Christ makes all the difference! **'To live is Christ.'** Think of Paul in prison. The chains hurt him. He is not free to go out. But look at him! Is he unhappy? Does he complain? No! He is full of joy because of Jesus. He talks about Jesus. He is in prison for Jesus. His life is about Jesus!

'To die is gain (will bring more).' Paul does not want to **run away** from life. No, but he really wants to go to be with Jesus! That will mean even more joy. Paul is not scared of death. Death is like a door that leads to Jesus.

❥ *Think about your life. What is it all about? For you, to live is…? Perhaps your life is full of things. Perhaps it is empty.*

❥ *Think about your death. Are you afraid? Why are people afraid?*

We cannot choose when we die, but we can choose **how we live**. Will you live for **Christ**? Only then will you be ready to die. You will not be afraid of death because death takes you home to Jesus!

JESUS OR ME?

Paul shows us how to make life choices. Paul may live or he may die, but he has chosen two things.

1. To honour Christ.
📖 *Philippians 1:19-20*

Paul knows that any day a guard may take him to the lions. But Paul is not worried. Think of that! Paul cares more about something else. He wants the courage to **honour Christ**. Jesus matters far more than whether Paul lives or dies.

2. To put others first.
📖 *Philippians 1:24-26*

Paul would love to die, but to him that seems rather selfish! The believers need him to live. Paul wants to go and enjoy Christ, but there is something even more important! He would prefer to help the Christians first. He would prefer to give **them** joy. He can wait to have his joy in heaven with Jesus!

❥ *Jesus or me? We make choices every day. Those choices show if I want to **honour Christ** or look after myself. My choices show whether I **put other people first**, or me first. [Talk more about those choices. Give examples.]*

STUDY: Philippians 1:27-30

6 GOSPEL FIGHT

◉ Background

Why has Paul said a lot about his own troubles?
Philippians 1:12-26

It is because he wants to help the Christians at Philippi with their difficulties! Paul has come to the main point of the chapter. He wants the Christians to fight for the truth about Jesus (the gospel) **as he** fights for the gospel.
Philippians 1:27-30

◉ Main point

Be like Paul! Live for the gospel, fight for the gospel, suffer for the gospel.

✦ Something to work on

This is a very helpful section for a preacher or a pastor. Pray about it a lot. Are you willing to spend your life like this? Is this how your church family thinks about the gospel? Do you help them to work together, so that more people hear about Jesus and live for Jesus?

◉ Notes

- **Philippians 1:27.** Our lives must be like the gospel that we talk about. Our lives must be full of love and truth because the gospel is full of love and truth.

- **Philippians 1:27.** When Paul comes to Philippi (or when he hears news of them), what will he find? Paul hopes to find people who fight ('contend', 'compete') **together** for the gospel. It is like a team sport. Everyone tries as hard as they can. They work **together** to win.

- **Philippians 1:28.** When we do not let the enemy frighten us, it shows two things. 1. It shows them that they will lose and God will punish them. 2. It shows that God has saved us and will keep us to the end.

- **Philippians 1:29.** It is a privilege (honour, a good thing) to suffer for Jesus! It is God's **gift**. God gives a Christian both **faith** and **suffering**.

- **Philippians 1:30.** Paul is in prison, but it is not only Paul who suffers! All God's people suffer together as they fight for the gospel.

➡ PREACH: Philippians 1:27-30

LIVE FOR THE GOSPEL
📖 *Philippians 1:27*

⊕ Sometimes the best sports players behave badly [think of an example]. Their bad behaviour makes that sport look bad.

- When Christians behave badly, what does it make people think about their message? What kinds of behaviour turn people away from Jesus?

Think how beautiful the good news about Jesus is. It is so full of love and truth and joy. **Our lives should be like the gospel!** They should be full of love and truth and joy.

» What pleases God? For us to have lots of gifts—or to be like Jesus? To talk a lot about Jesus—or to live like our message?

FIGHT FOR THE GOSPEL
📖 *Philippians 1:27*

⊕ Imagine that you are in a race. There is a big prize. [Describe how hard you would try to win!]

We should try even harder for the gospel! And we do not race alone. We struggle as a team, together. We must not give up. We must not start to say unkind things about each other. We must not hurt each other. No, we can never win the race like that! The gospel of Jesus is so important that we must stand together. Then the people round us can know the truth about Jesus.

*» How much does the gospel matter to you? Are you willing to **work together** so that people hear about Jesus? Will you let quarrels or jealous thoughts stop you?*

SUFFER FOR THE GOSPEL
📖 *Philippians 1:28-30*

The devil is against the gospel. So people on Satan's side are against the gospel. They will attack Christians who stand for the gospel. Paul says three things to encourage us when we suffer for Jesus—

1. It is a **sign**; Philippians 1:28. People may be against us because we follow Jesus. But that shows that we are true Christians. It shows that we will win and our enemies will lose.

2. It is a **gift**; Philippians 1:29. It is God's good gift to believe in Jesus. It is also God's good gift to suffer for Him! 📖 *Matthew 5:10-12.*

3. It is **normal**; Philippians 1:30. Paul, in prison, wants to encourage the believers. 'It is OK to suffer! Do not give up—we are in the battle together!'

STUDY: Philippians 2:1-4

7 THINK THE SAME

▪ Background

Paul tells these Christians his reason to live. He lives for **Christ**! (Philippians 1:21) He lives for the **gospel**! (Philippians 1:12, 16, 18, 25)

Paul wants them (and us) to live for **Christ** and for the **gospel** (Philippians 1:27).

But two kinds of things can stop this—

- **Outside attack.** People who are not Christians try to hurt us.
  Philippians 1:27-30

- **Inside attack.** Christians hurt each other.
  Philippians 2:1-4, 4:2-3

▪ Main point

Think the same! (Put Christ and the gospel first). Then you will love each other well.

★ Something to work on

What things divide the Christians in your church? Many of these things are very small. They are not important. They are not about the true message of Jesus. How can you help people to see this?

When we care most about Christ and the gospel, we love each other. And the little things no longer matter much.

▪ Notes

- **Philippians 2:1.** 'If you have…' (some translations). This means '**Because** you have all these blessings… then think the same'.

- **Philippians 2:3.** Do nothing to make you feel proud. Be humble. Think that other people are more important than you are.

- **Philippians 2:4.** 'Interests' means 'benefit' or 'advantage'. Do things that help other people, not only you!

→ PREACH: Philippians 2:1-4

THE DANGER
Philippians 2:3

⊕ When you vote for a politician, what do you care about? Do you want the person who will be fair, who will care for the poor people? Or do you want the one who will give **you** more money?

It is so easy to be selfish! But Jesus has changed his people. Christians no longer care most about themselves. But the devil wants us to forget this. He wants us to be selfish and ambitious and proud in our church.

» *[It may help to talk about this in groups.]*

- In what ways does **proud thinking** show among God's people?
- What are the results?

Stop to think and pray. Ask God to forgive you and to change you.

THE ANSWER
Philippians 2:2-4

The most important thing we need to learn is to **think right.** We will never live right until we think right.

Paul wants all Christians everywhere to think the same! The same spirit, the same purpose, the same desires, the same love!

He wants believers to think that Jesus is everything! He wants us to think that everyone must hear the gospel about Jesus. He wants us to think that we are not important. He wants us to think that other Christians are important.

Then we will be united and humble and loving. Together we will live for Jesus. Remember *Philippians 1:27.*

THE REASON
Philippians 2:1

Why should we live like Philippians 2:2-4? Why not be selfish?

Because we know Jesus! (Philippians 2:1)

[Talk about these four things that all true Christians know.]

These gifts from God have changed us—we cannot still be so selfish and proud! God has given us so much—we want to give him everything we have!

» *Pray that God's generous love to you will make you more humble and loving.*

Perhaps you have never truly known Jesus like this. Ask him to change you.

STUDY: Philippians 2:5-11

8 — THINK LIKE JESUS!

▣ Background

One of Paul's big desires for these Christians is for them to **think right**. He has **prayed** about this (Philippians 1:9-10). He has told them how **he** thinks because he wants them to copy him (Philippians 1:12-26). He has asked them to think right (Philippians 2:1-4).

Now Paul points us to Jesus. We need to think like Christ. We need to have his attitude.

📖 *Philippians 2:5-11*

▣ Main point

Think like Jesus. He was humble. He gave everything to save his people.

✦ Something to work on

This section is all about Jesus. We want people to love and worship him. But do not forget the main point! Paul says all this because **we need to be like Jesus.** Like Jesus, we need to humble ourselves and serve other people.

▣ Notes

- **Philippians 2:6-7.** Jesus is God. He owns heaven's glory. But he did not hold on to that. He let go of everything and became a baby. Of course Jesus was still God! But he lived as a human, with nothing.

- **Philippians 2:7.** 'The nature of a servant.' Jesus came to serve. He gave up his rights. He did not come as a special person. He came as a servant.

- **Philippians 2:8.** The cross was the 'lowest' place, the place of most shame. Jesus died like the worst person. (See also Galatians 3:13.)

- **Philippians 2:9.** Jesus deserves the highest honour **because** he went to the lowest place. The **cross** brings Jesus the most praise! The most painful thing was the **best** thing Jesus ever did (Revelation 5:12).

- **Philippians 2:10-11.** This does not mean that everyone will love Jesus. Even people who hate him will have to fall on their knees ('bow') and worship him!

➡ PREACH: Philippians 2:5-11

[Start with some songs which praise and honour Jesus.]

THINK LIKE JESUS
📖 *Philippians 2:5-8*

[⊞ Tell a story about someone who has a very important position. This person becomes very humble. He does a job that nobody else is willing to do.]

Now think who Jesus is! Creator! God! All the angels worship him!

Jesus came from the highest place in heaven to the lowest place on earth! He gave up everything to become nothing. [Talk about Jesus willing to be a baby, willing to go to the cross.] Jesus deserves everyone to worship him! But people spat on him and laughed at him and killed him.

Jesus chose to do this! He chose to be a servant! Praise him!

» *Think like Jesus.* **Think like a servant.** *And copy Jesus.*
📖 *Philippians 2:5. Be glad to be nothing.*
[Give examples. Talk about how this will show in our lives.]

• **Why** did Jesus do all this? What was he thinking?

It was the only way to **save people**! This is why Jesus became nothing. He loved sinners that much! He was willing to go to the cross like a criminal. Praise and love him!

» *So will you be willing to do the worst jobs in the church? Will you be humble and put other people first? If not, what does that show about you?*

GLORY TO JESUS
📖 *Philippians 2:9-11*

Who does God honour? He honours Jesus, because he let go of everything and became a servant!

⊞ How does your village or town honour a man who risks his life to rescue a child? Jesus **gave** his life to save all his children from hell! How we should honour Jesus! How the Father honours Jesus!
📖 *Philippians 2:9-11*

» *Do you praise and honour Jesus? Do not leave it too late. Do not leave it until the day you will **have** to fall on your knees and worship Jesus. Everyone will honour Jesus when he returns. This is not because they all want to. But God will make sure that Jesus gets the honour that he deserves.*

What about your life now? Jesus deserves a life full of praise! He deserves praise for ever and ever. How will this show in our lives?

STUDY: Philippians 2:12-18

9 SALVATION SHINES

◉ Background

Paul's big point is 📖 *Philippians 1:27*. Paul wants them (and us) to live for Christ and for the gospel.

So Paul gives us the best example, Jesus. 📖 *Philippians 2:1-11*.

Now Paul comes back to his big point. 📖 *Philippians 2:12-18*. He says 'so then' or 'therefore' (Philippians 2:12). He means: **'Because of Jesus** (Philippians 2:1-11), you should live like this. He saved you—the salvation that he gave you should shine out.'

◉ Main point

God's gift of salvation shows. Make sure that it shines out in your lives!

◉ Something to work on

In Philippians 2:12, Paul does not mean that we must work to earn our salvation! Salvation is God's gift. Jesus **completely** saves his people through the cross. Nothing that we do helps to save us.

However, God's gift of salvation is active! It is not like a gift that we hide away in a safe place. It is a gift to use. It is a gift that will change us. We must not be lazy with that gift. We must work at it. We must shine out like stars.

◉ Notes

- **Philippians 2:12.** 'With fear and trembling.' Christians do not need to be afraid of God. But we should hate to do anything that makes God sad. Salvation is such a great gift. We must be careful to live as people that God has saved.

- **Philippians 2:15.** 'Crooked and depraved generation.' The world around us is corrupt (not honest) and evil. Christians must be completely different.

- **Philippians 2:16.** The 'day of Christ' is when Jesus comes back. Paul will see that these believers followed Jesus to the end. Then all his hard work will be worth it.

- **Philippians 2:17-18.** Paul thinks that the Roman king, Caesar, may kill him. He imagines his life given up to God like an Old Testament offering. He means this: 'I am happy to die if it is for you. If I have done a little to help your faith, then I am glad to pay the price of death. Do not be sad, but praise God!'

➡ PREACH: Philippians 2:12-18

WORK AT YOUR SALVATION!
📖 *Philippians 2:12-14*

✠ Imagine that you receive a big gift. A cow! This will give you a good income. So what will you do? Will you be lazy and do nothing for your cow? Or will you work hard so that your cow gives you milk every day?

This is a bit like God's gift, salvation. Like the cow, it is free! And, like the cow, we must not be lazy with it! God wants his salvation gift to work in our lives.

- What things does God want Christians to work at? (Examples: 📖 Philippians 2:14, 16.) Do you find this easy?

📖 *Philippians 2:13*

This is good news. God does not leave us to work on our own. He works with us and in us! He has a big plan for us. He plans to make us pure and holy, like Jesus. So he changes us on the inside. He helps us to tell the truth, to show love, to control our anger. The biggest problem can be that we do not **want** to change. But God can make us willing to change.

- Christians have a special gift—salvation. They have special help—God himself! How should this make us feel, as we work to please God (Philippians 2:12)?

SALVATION THAT SHINES!
📖 *Philippians 2:15-16*

✠ I have a broken lamp on my desk. It is no good. It does not work!

If our salvation works, we will shine out in the darkness.

1. Salvation shines by PURE LIVES; 📖 *Philippians 2:15*

❱❱ Do Christians in your church live like stars shining in the darkness? Or do you do the same things as people round you?

- *What are the things that you find hardest? How can you live to please God when everyone else takes bribes, or uses his wife badly, or lies, or…?*

2. Salvation shines out GOD'S WORDS; 📖 *Philippians 2:16*

We have a message that brings life! We cannot keep that message quiet.

❱❱ Have you received God's gift of salvation? **Then do not keep it for yourself!** Offer it out to people who still live in the dark.

It is often easy to **say** that we are Christians. But Paul wants these Christians to have a salvation that is active. How important is it to him?

📖 *Philippians 2:16-17*

STUDY: Philippians 2:19-24

10 A GOOD EXAMPLE

◉ Background

Paul expects to find out soon if he will die, or be free from prison. Paul is happy to die for Jesus. If he does die, he wants the Philippian Christians to have joy.

📖 *Philippians 2:17-18*

But he also knows how much these Christians care for him. He wants to send them news quickly. Who will he send? Timothy and Epaphroditus.

📖 *Philippians 2:19-30*

These two Christians are very good examples. Their lives show what Paul has taught in Philippians 2. They are humble servants, like Jesus. They give themselves for the gospel. They shine out like stars. Paul wants the Philippian believers to copy Timothy and Epaphroditus.

◉ Main point

Timothy is a good example. He does not care most about himself. He cares about other people, about Jesus and about the gospel.

★ Something to work on

Everyone except Timothy was too busy with their own lives. They did not put Christ and the gospel first. Think of your own life. What would Paul have said about you? How much do you really care for the church that God has given you to serve?

◉ Notes

- **Philippians 2:19.** This shows how much Paul cared about these believers. They wanted news about Paul, but he wanted news about them!

- **Philippians 2:21.** See Philippians 2:4-5. 'Interests' (or 'affairs') means 'benefit', 'advantage'. Sadly, Timothy was the only one who really wanted to do things that helped Jesus, not himself!

- **Philippians 2:22.** 'Proved himself.' Timothy had shown that he was true and genuine. For years, he served the Lord with Paul. Timothy took the message of Jesus to Philippi with Paul (Acts 16:1-3, 12).

- **Philippians 2:24.** Paul was ready to die. But he expected Caesar to set him free. Then he wanted to visit the Philippian Christians.

➲ PREACH: Philippians 2:19-24

❥ *Who is willing to help? Who is willing to go? Are you?*

One day God made Linda think about her life. Then she answered God—'I will do anything you say. I will go anywhere you want.'

Are you willing to say that to God?

JESUS FIRST
📖 *Philippians 2:20-21*

[Talk about excuses. 'I am not able to help because…']

Why do we give excuses? Often it is because we put **ourselves first**. If we help, we will have to work hard, or we will miss something we wanted to do, or…

For Timothy, it means a long, hard journey. 800 dangerous miles! So did he give excuses? Why not?
📖 *Philippians 2:20-21*

Timothy was the **only one** willing to go. Think how sad Paul felt. It is easy to say that Jesus comes first. But only Timothy put Jesus first in action.

When we put Jesus first, we really care about **other people**. We so much want the best for them. We do not mind what it costs us.

❥ *Not many people are like Timothy. Will you pray that you will be like him?*

❥ *What will this mean in practice? How can you show that you care for other Christians?*

A TRUSTED SERVANT
📖 *Philippians 2:22*

⊕ Do you worry, after you ask someone to do an important job? 'Will he be honest?' 'Will she give up when it is hard?' 'Will he do it well?'

Paul did not worry about Timothy! He knew that he could trust him. Why?

Timothy had travelled with Paul on his journeys. They faced many dangers together as they told people about Jesus. Paul gave Timothy many difficult jobs. But Timothy never disappointed him. He was like a son to Paul.

Timothy had proved himself. He was a faithful servant of Jesus.

❥ *Would you like to be like Timothy? A trusted servant of Jesus?*

Think how you can begin. Start with little things, things that no one else wants to do. When you say that you will do something, be sure to do it. And always do it well, for Jesus.

STUDY: Philippians 2:25-30

11 ANOTHER GOOD EXAMPLE

▪ Background

Paul has used many examples to help us to **think** right and **live** right.

- Paul himself—Philippians 1:12-26
- Jesus—Philippians 2:5-11
- Timothy—Philippians 2:19-24
- And Epaphroditus— *Philippians 2:25-30*

Later, Paul tells us to copy these examples; *Philippians 3:17*

Also, Paul wants the Philippian Christians to **respect** Epaphroditus.

▪ Main point

Respect people like Epaphroditus. (Think highly of them. Give them honour.) Respect people who risk their lives for the work of Christ.

★ Something to work on

It is easy for us to respect the wrong kind of people. We may respect people because they have money, or gifts, or power. We may respect people just because they speak well. How can you help your listeners think right about who to respect? How can your church respect the kind of people that God respects?

▪ Notes

- **Philippians 2:25.** Epaphroditus was from the church at Philippi. They sent him to Paul, in prison in Rome, with love gifts. Epaphroditus became very ill but was now better. So Paul sends him back to Philippi with Timothy and with this letter.

- **Philippians 2:25.** 'Fellow-worker' (worker-with-me) and 'fellow-soldier' (soldier-with-me). Paul shows Epaphroditus respect with these names. Epaphroditus has truly shared in the battle for the gospel.

- **Philippians 2:26.** Epaphroditus was very ill, but see who **he** thinks about! He was upset because the Philippian Christians would worry about him!

- **Philippians 2:30.** Paul reminds the Philippians that Epaphroditus risked his life for Christ and for **them**. He carried **their** gift! (See Philippians 2:25.)

➡ PREACH: Philippians 2:25-30

DEAR BROTHER
📖 *Philippians 2:25*

Epaphroditus was an ordinary Christian. He probably had an ordinary job. The Bible does not say that he preached or had great gifts.

But look how Paul values him! The great apostle calls this ordinary Christian 'brother'! Paul has great respect for Epaphroditus because he risked his life to visit Paul.

> *You do not need great gifts, like Paul or Timothy, to serve Christ. You can be a young person or a very old person and be Paul's 'brother'. You just need to be willing to **do what you can** for Jesus.*

FAITHFUL SERVANT
📖 *Philippians 2:25, 30*

The church needed someone to take their gift to Paul. So Epaphroditus went. Perhaps other people could not go. Perhaps some were not willing. But Epaphroditus was willing to go for his church and for Christ.

- What does Philippians 2:26 show? How does Epaphroditus feel about the Christians back home?

> *Most people are willing to help when it is their own idea, their own interest.*

> *Are you willing to be a servant for the church, **whatever** the job?*

READY TO TAKE RISKS
📖 *Philippians 2:30*

⊕ Talk about a dangerous sport. Some people love it. Other people want to stay safe! They do not want to risk a broken leg or…

Gospel work is dangerous! Christians who love the gospel take risks. Epaphroditus risked his life to encourage Paul in prison. He nearly died. But he was happy to do that for Jesus.

Once, people risked their lives to preach Jesus in your country. Perhaps they do today. [Tell true stories if you know them. Talk about the kinds of risks we need to take today.]

> *Epaphroditus is a great example. He was an ordinary Christian who put Jesus first and loved the gospel. Think of people like that who you know.*

- *Respect them! (Philippians 2:29). They may not have important positions, but God values them. Talk about who we should respect and why.]*
- *Copy them! Spend time with them. Pray with them. Ask them to teach you to put Jesus first.*

STUDY: Philippians 3:1-7

12 I AM SURE

▪ Background
Paul wants us to look for good examples. He wants us to copy people who live for Jesus. Paul also wants us to watch out for **bad** examples.

At Philippi, some people taught false things. They were Jews who said that to be a true Christian you **also** had to be a Jew. They said that you had to be circumcised, like a Jew.

So Paul tells how he learned to trust Jesus to save him.

📖 *Philippians 3:1-11*

▪ Main point
Do not trust your own efforts to make you right with God. Be confident (sure) about Jesus.

▪ Something to work on
Your listeners may not be Jews, but many of them may have similar wrong ideas. Some are sure that they are Christians because they go to church. Many people think that the way to please God is to try harder. And some true Christians are not completely sure that they will go to heaven.

They all need to hear the same thing. We **can** be sure, when we trust Jesus **alone** to save us.

▪ Notes
- **Philippians 3:1.** 'Rejoice'; 'be joyful.' This does not only mean 'be happy'. Paul means 'be confident in Jesus; be glad that you are safe in Jesus'.

- **Philippians 3:2.** 'Dogs.' Paul uses strong words against these false teachers. They say that Christians must be circumcised, like Jews. So Paul calls them 'mutilators of the flesh'. (Circumcision is when someone cuts off a boy's foreskin.)

- **Philippians 3:3.** Circumcision was a mark to show that Jews belonged to God. But God's true people (Christians) have the mark of God's Spirit! This shows that they belong to God. This is the 'true circumcision'. They do not trust their own efforts at religion ('the flesh'). They have joy because Jesus has done everything.

- **Philippians 3:4-6.** Paul had been the best Jew possible. He did all the right things! He was sure that God was pleased with him. But he was wrong.

- **Philippians 3:7.** Then Paul saw the truth. All his 'good marks' with God ('profit') were nothing. Christ is everything.

➡ PREACH: Philippians 3:1-7

SURE—AND WRONG
📖 *Philippians 3:4-7*

⊕ You answer all the questions in an exam. You come out pleased. You are sure that you have done well. But when the results come, you find that you failed the exam. How does that feel?

When Paul was a young Jew, he was very sure of himself. He came from a good family of Jews. He studied the Old Testament well. He kept all the Jewish laws. He gave his whole life to God. He was sure that God was pleased with him.

But Paul was completely wrong. Imagine that you worked hard for three years. All you did was study for the exam. Then your mark was 0 out of 100! It was like that for Paul. God was not pleased **at all** with all Paul's efforts. It was as if he got **less** than 0. Now, Paul counts all his efforts for God as a **loss**.
📖 *Philippians 3:7*

> ❯❯ *Think about your life. Think of the good things you have done. Think of all the reasons why God may decide not to punish you, but to forgive you [give examples]. Add them all up. Have you done enough to be saved?*

❯❯ *They are all nothing! They do not help to save you **at all**. They make God sad, not happy. **All those things are the wrong way to be forgiven by God**. What we do does not get us to heaven.*

SURE—AND RIGHT
📖 *Philippians 3:1-3*

Paul is still sure—but now he is right! God has shown Paul the right way to please him—through Jesus.

So he says 'Rejoice in the **Lord**'. True Christians are people who are sure about Jesus. They are confident in Jesus, not themselves.

⊕ It is as if Jesus takes the exam for believers! We are full of sin. We have failed to please God. But we **know** that Jesus scores 100. It is as if Jesus tears up our terrible exam paper and puts his perfect one in its place.

Paul describes a true Christian in 📖 *Philippians 3:3*. [Talk more about it. Show how we must not trust our own efforts at religion. We must only trust our perfect Saviour.]

> ❯❯ *Do you only trust Jesus to save you? Then you can be **sure**—and forgiven. Be joyful in Jesus—he can never fail you.*

STUDY: Philippians 3:8-11

13 TO KNOW JESUS

▣ Background

Paul wants us to hold on to our faith in Jesus alone. Nothing else matters. Once, Paul was proud because he was a good Jew. Now he sees that is worth nothing.

📖 *Philippians 3:1-7*

Jesus is everything to Paul. Now that he knows Jesus, Paul only wants to know him better. And he wants us to think the same!

📖 *Philippians 3:8-11*

▣ Main point

If you know Jesus, you have everything. You will only want to know Jesus more and more!

▣ Something to work on

Do not misunderstand Paul. He no longer tries to be right with God by his good works. He now trusts Jesus for that. In Philippians 3:9, Paul shows that we get right with God by **faith**.

Paul tells us here what he **values**. He **wants very much** to know Jesus more and more. All Paul's efforts to be good are like rubbish. Jesus is everything.

▣ Notes

- **Philippians 3:8.** Once, Paul was so proud of the things he did (Philippians 3:5-6). Now, he can throw it all away. It did not help him know God! It is like rubbish (or 'refuse'). The only valuable thing is to know Jesus—because Jesus is the way to God.

- **Philippians 3:9.** 'Found (united) in him.' Paul says that he is with Jesus. Before, Paul trusted his good works. Now, he trusts Jesus. Paul's 'righteousness' ('goodness' or 'the way God accepts him') is from Jesus. It is a gift from God, which Paul has received by faith.

- **Philippians 3:10.** 'The power of his resurrection.' Christians have a risen Saviour! We can know Jesus' power in our lives. Jesus' power defeats our sin, so that we can know Jesus better (Ephesians 3:16-19).

- **Philippians 3:11.** One day Paul will also rise from the dead. He does not doubt this. But he looks forward to it so much. Then he will know Jesus as he wants to!

➡ PREACH: Philippians 3:8-11

TO KNOW JESUS
📖 *Philippians 3:8-9*

Once, Paul did not know Jesus. He **hated** Jesus! He did not need Jesus! Paul thought that his own life was good enough to please God. Then, all of a sudden, everything changed. [Tell the story, from Acts 22:6-16.]

> ❯❯ *Has God changed you? He may have changed you much more slowly than he changed Paul. But, like Paul, do you know Jesus now? If so, then—*

1. Jesus means everything to you. If Paul lost everything he owned, what would he have left? He would still have everything, because Jesus is everything! Is Philippians 3:8 true for you too?

2. Jesus is the way God accepts you; 📖 *Philippians 3:9.* This is why Jesus is everything! Our own 'righteousness' is no good. We may think we are 'right' before God, but God will never accept our efforts. But God **has accepted Jesus**! Now God does not look at Paul's good works. He looks at Jesus instead of Paul! So God is pleased with Paul because of Jesus.

> ❯❯ *Do you know Jesus by faith? Does God accept **you** because of what Jesus has done? He does if you have **faith** in Jesus. God **gives** us 'righteousness' when we trust in Jesus.*

TO KNOW JESUS MORE AND MORE
📖 *Philippians 3:10-11*

⊕ Imagine that you just ate the best meal ever! Imagine that it was free, and you could have another one any time. Would you come back?

Paul knows Jesus. Jesus completely satisfies him. But Paul is not full up! He wants to come again and again to Jesus. He wants to know Jesus better. Are you like this? He tells us two things he wants to know more of—

1. More of Jesus' power. Think how much power Jesus has! Think how much power it took to rise from the dead! Paul wants to know more of this power himself. But **not** so that he can do astonishing miracles. Paul wants Jesus' power to **change** him, to make him more like Jesus. Then Paul will know Jesus better. Is that what you want most too?

2. More of Jesus' suffering. Paul does not enjoy pain! But he wants to get close to Jesus. To get close to someone we must share a little in their pain. You cannot suffer on a cross like Jesus, but you can hate sin, you can feel Jesus' pain at evil. And you can be willing to suffer, as you share the good news about Jesus.

> ❯❯ *We come back for good food—but do we come back for more of Jesus?*

35

STUDY: Philippians 3:12-16

14 RUN THE RACE

◉ Background

Paul wants us to think like Jesus. He wants us to live for the gospel.

He has warned us of a danger—

Do not be like the Jews and try hard to earn God's blessing (Philippians 3:1-7).

There is another, opposite danger. We must not say 'Jesus has done everything for us. So we sit down and do nothing.' No! Paul wants us to try hard, like him. He wants us to run the Christian race!

Philippians 3:8-16

◉ Main point

Run the race right to the end. Try very hard to live for Jesus.

◉ Something to work on

We must not think that Paul wants to **earn** the prize. He knows that Jesus has already won the prize for him! **Jesus** took hold of Paul (Philippians 3:12). **God** called him to heaven (Philippians 3:14).

But God has called Christians to **run the race.** Jesus is not a taxi that takes us to heaven. Jesus calls us to follow him in the hard race. Then we will receive the prize, which Jesus won for us!

◉ Notes

- **Philippians 3:12-13.** Paul uses very strong words to say how hard he runs. He is like a runner in the Olympic Games. He says 'I press on', or 'strive' (try very hard). He 'strains' forwards, like a runner who leans forward to reach the winning line.

- **Philippians 3:14.** The prize is to be with Jesus in heaven. God chose Paul for that prize. But this letter shows that Paul does not think only about himself. Paul does not mean to arrive in heaven **alone**. God chose Paul to bring all these dear believers along with him. As Paul runs, he holds hands with these Christians.

- **Philippians 3:15-16.** Paul knows that not all Christians run well. He does not want us to give up. He wants us all to think like him, but he knows that many Christians are weak. He tells us to go forward even so! We will learn more as we go.

➔ PREACH: Philippians 3:12-16

ONE THING
📖 *Philippians 3:12-13*

⊕ Talk about Paul's picture of a runner in a race. Describe how hard she tries to win, how she stretches every muscle. The runner only thinks about **one thing**. She must win the race.

» We can have so many things to do that we can forget to run the race. We forget the one most important thing! The one thing that really matters is to live for Jesus. [Discuss the things that get in the way, and stop us from living to please Jesus. Pray that you may be like Paul.]

Look carefully and you will see that this is a not just a race but a chase! First Jesus chased Paul—and caught him. Now Paul chases Jesus—all the way to heaven.

» Do you remember the time when Jesus chased you? He wanted you to belong to him. He wanted to bring you home to him. And his love touched your heart and made you want to follow him. Chase Jesus now! Do one thing: keep close to Jesus!

FORGET THE PAST
📖 *Philippians 3:13*

Many things in the past can make us sad and weak. Then we may feel that we are no good. We cannot carry on in the race. What do you find hard to forget?

If we have trusted Jesus, he has forgiven all our mistakes and sins. We need to forget them because Jesus has forgotten them! Jesus has taken all our sins away at the cross. (Isaiah 43:25)

REMEMBER THE PRIZE
📖 *Philippians 3:14*

Some Christians seem to think that they are such good Christians! They think that they have nothing left to learn! So they stop running hard. What does Paul think?
📖 *Philippians 3:12.*

Paul is not there yet. He has plenty to learn. He wants to be more like Jesus. So Paul runs on and on. He keeps his eye on the prize.

The prize is to be with Jesus forever. Not just me but all my brothers and sisters in Jesus. We race together. We help each other, so that we all get that prize. [Talk about how wonderful it will be.]
📖 *2 Timothy 4:7-8*

» Do not look at all the money and possessions you can have now. They will stop you from running! Look up to the prize. And run for Jesus!

STUDY: Philippians 3:17-4:1

15 TWO WAYS TO FOLLOW

▪ Background

In this letter, Paul gives many good examples to follow. (Paul, Jesus, Timothy, Epaphroditus.) He also warns about bad examples who teach the wrong thing (Philippians 3:2).

Here he sums up all of that. He says 'Follow the right people'.

📖 *Philippians 3:12 – 4:1*

▪ Main point

Follow the right way. Live like people who belong to heaven.

✦ Something to work on

Paul writes to Christians, but do all your listeners know Jesus? Ask them to look at these two kinds of people. They live in two opposite ways and end up in two opposite places. Who do they want to be like?

▪ Notes

- **Philippians 3:17.** Paul has shown these Christians a 'pattern' ('example'). That means a way of life that they should follow.

- **Philippians 3:18.** See Philippians 3:2. These people (Jews) say that they love God! But they say that it is not enough to trust Jesus. They say that you have to be a Jew too. Many people today teach that you have to do **more** than trust in Jesus' death. Paul calls them enemies of the cross.

- **Philippians 3:19.** 'Their destiny is destruction'—they will end up in hell.

'Their god is their stomach'—they only want things that satisfy the desires of their bodies (food, sex, fun…)

'Their glory is in their shame'—they are proud of what they should be ashamed of.

- **Philippians 3:20.** 'Citizens of heaven.' That means that our home country is heaven. Christians are foreigners here on earth. We should live like people who belong to heaven.

- **Philippians 3:21.** One day Jesus will come back. His power will change our poor weak bodies. Jesus will give believers bodies like his own body (1 Corinthians 15:49-52).

➡ PREACH: Philippians 3:17 - 4:1

THE WRONG PEOPLE TO GO WITH
📖 *Philippians 3:18-19*

Be very careful how you choose your friends. Jesus does want Christians to be good friends to people who are not yet Christians. But he does not want us to copy them. He does not want us to live like them. He wants us to show them the right way to go.

Why is Paul crying? Many people who seem like good people are in fact enemies of the cross! They may go to church, but they do not want to trust the Saviour who died for our sins. Their lives show that they are not on Jesus' side.

- What four things does Paul say about them in 📖 *Philippians 3:19*? [Talk about each one.]

⏩ *Do you know people like this? Maybe you like to watch them on television. Perhaps you are like them. Do not follow these people! You will end up in hell.*
📖 *Matthew 7:13-14.*

If you are a Christian, be careful who you marry. Perhaps you are afraid of being lonely. But never marry someone who is not in love with Jesus. Do not even start a close friendship with him or her. They will take you the wrong way.

THE RIGHT PEOPLE TO GO WITH
📖 *Philippians 3:17, 19-21*

Most people go down the wide, popular road that leads to hell. But a few of us go along a narrow, difficult path. Everyone else thinks we are strange. This is what we are like—

1. WE ARE CITIZENS OF HEAVEN;
📖 *Philippians 3:20.* ✚ Imagine that you have a passport that says you were born in heaven! It is like that. Christians are heaven-people who must live on earth for a while.

- What difference will it make, when you remember that?

2. WE WAIT FOR JESUS;
📖 *Philippians 3:20.* We remember that Jesus promised to come back. We are excited because he will take us home!

3. WE WAIT FOR JESUS TO CHANGE US; 📖 *Philippians 3:21.* It is hard to be in pain, to be lonely, to be poor. But we will not be like this for long! Jesus will change our weak bodies. He will make us like him.

⏩ *There are two kinds of people. People whose lives are all about this world and themselves. And people whose lives are all about heaven and Jesus. How will **you** live?*
📖 *Philippians 4:1*

STUDY: Philippians 4:2-5

16 DO IT!

◉ Background

In Philippians 1 – 3, Paul teaches about the way Christians should think. He wants us to follow the right examples. He wants us to live for Jesus.

In Philippians 4, Paul shows how this works **in real life**. The first thing to put right is a quarrel. Two women need to think like Jesus.

📖 *Philippians 2:1-5, 4:1-5*

◉ Main points

Stop quarrels. Have joy in the Lord. Have a gentle attitude.

✶ Something to work on

Are there Christians in your church who are like these two women? Perhaps they do not even speak to each other. Paul shows us that it is very important not to close your eyes to problems like this. Pray that God's word will speak to these people. Also, think who may be able to help them. Do not let quarrels continue. They bring shame on Jesus and stop the gospel.

◉ Notes

- **Philippians 4:2.** Paul used a strong word ('plead'; 'beg') to ask these women to agree. Also, the letter was read out in public! It is very important to sort out quarrels!

- **Philippians 4:3.** These women had worked ('contended') with Paul to spread the gospel! It is so sad that they quarrelled. See how Paul asks someone else to help them. His name probably means 'yoke-fellow' ('partner').

- **Philippians 4:5.** 'Gentleness.' This does not mean 'weak'. It means kind and caring. It means to think more about other people than ourselves.

  📖 *Philippians 2:3, 14; James 3:17-18.*

- **Philippians 4:5.** 'The Lord is near.' This may mean that Jesus is here with us. Or it may mean that Jesus will come back soon. Both are true. Both are important to remember.

➡ PREACH: Philippians 4:2-5

STOP QUARRELS!
📖 *Philippians 4:2-3*

⊕ Two famous football managers hate each other. The newspapers talk about it. One of them has stored up all the things the other one has said. He wants to make trouble for him. But this is bad for football. Football should be a friendly game, not a war!

❥ *Are you like that? Have you stored up things in your head against someone? Do you say bad things about them? Or perhaps you stay away from them. If you are a Christian, this brings shame on Jesus. It makes people think that our message of God's love is not true. God's word says to us 'It must stop!' What can you do to put right any quarrels you may have?*

- What had these two women done in the past? Now what do they do?
- They must stop their quarrels. What things does Paul do to help them?

Perhaps you can be a peace-maker and help other Christians.

JOY IN THE LORD!
📖 *Philippians 4:4*

⊕ These are not easy words for Paul to say! Some years ago, he and Silas were in prison in Philippi. The guard beat them. It hurt a lot. Yet they sang songs of praise to God! (Acts 16:22-25)

Now Paul is in prison again. The chains hurt him. But he still says 'Be full of joy!'

- How can he be full of joy? How can we **always** have this joy?

Christian joy does not come from **things that happen to us**. We do not have this joy when things are good and feel miserable when things are bad. No, Christian joy is **in the Lord**. Whatever happens to us, Jesus is our same wonderful Lord.

- What things about Jesus mean that you can **always** have joy in him?

BE GENTLE!
📖 *Philippians 4:5*

Christians should not be difficult to get on with. They should not be proud of their own ideas and order people about. Sometimes we do need to say strong things, but we must be careful. We need to be kind and gentle, like Jesus.

What happens when someone who you respect walks into the room? Does it change the way you speak? Then remember that Jesus is already in the room! And one day soon, Jesus will come back for his people. Do not be ashamed when he comes.

STUDY: Philippians 4:6-7

17 WORRY MEDICINE

▣ Background

Paul wants us to think like Christians in every day life. This means—

- Agree with each other in the Lord (Philippians 4:2-3).
- Have joy in the Lord always (Philippians 4:4).
- Be gentle with people (Philippians 4:5).

It also changes what we do with our worries; *Philippians 4:6-7*.

▣ Main point

Trust God with your worries. Then God promises his peace.

▣ Something to work on

Remember that this promise of peace is not for everyone. It is for people who belong to Jesus. If we do not trust Jesus to save us, we **should** worry very much. God tells us there is no peace for us. Tell your listeners to bring their sins to the cross to find peace with God.

▣ Notes

- **Philippians 4:6.** Paul does not only say 'pray'. He uses three other words to help us pray rightly.

   'Petition'—this is humble asking. We deserve nothing, but we come to a great God.

   'Thanksgiving'—a good way to stop your worries is to thank God for all he has done for you.

   'Requests'—this means that we ask God for what we actually need. We say more than 'God, I feel worried'. We ask him what we need him to do about it.

- **Philippians 4:7.** 'Transcends.' God's peace is more than we can understand.

- **Philippians 4:7.** 'Guard.' The people of Philippi knew all about guards. Philippi was a Roman city. Many Roman soldiers guarded the city. Paul says that God's peace is like those Roman guards. It keeps us safe. It keeps out our enemies, our fears.

➡ PREACH: Philippians 4:6-7

TAKE THE MEDICINE
📖 *Philippians 4:6*

⊕ Imagine that you could buy worry medicine at the drug store. You may not expect it to work very well. Worry is too big a problem for medicine.

But God promises that his worry medicine **does** work. It works better than we can understand. But **we do need to take the medicine**. Listen well to what God tells us.

1. 'Do not worry.' When a friend says that, it does not usually help! But remember that **God** says this to us. We make God sad when we continue to worry, because he tells us not to.

- What if we have a very big problem? Is it OK to go on worrying then?

2. 'Do pray.' God does not only say 'Do not worry'. He gives us the medicine to take. He tells Christians what to do instead of worry. He wants us to give all our worries to him. [Talk about the things Paul says about how to pray—see Notes. Why is each one important to help us not to worry?]

God is our Father. He will look after us. We can be like a little child. We can put our little hands in his big hands and know that we are safe.
📖 *Matthew 6:25-34*

⊕ Imagine that you have a money problem. You go to your friend with all the bills. You talk about it for two hours. He listens. You feel better. Then you go home with all the bills. Does that stop your worry? No, you still have the money problem! You need to find someone who can **do** something about your problem.

When we pray, we do not come just to talk about our problems. We trust God to **look after** our problems. Leave them with God! Do not give him the worry when you pray, then take it back again when you stop! 📖 *1 Peter 5:7.*

» *Take God's worry medicine!*
📖 *Philippians 4:6. Will you obey God's word? Some of us find it hard, but God **will** help us when we follow what he says.*

RECEIVE GOD'S PEACE
📖 *Philippians 4:7*

[Ask people to tell about times of worry, when God has given them his peace.]

It does not matter how bad things are. It does not matter how afraid you are. God's peace is much stronger. It is his special peace. We cannot explain it. It keeps out the worries, just as guards keep out the enemy.

God keeps his promises. You take his medicine—he gives his peace.

STUDY: Philippians 4:8-9

18 THINK RIGHT, DO RIGHT

Background

In this letter, Paul has taught us how to **think right**. When we think right, we will live right. Paul has given us many examples to copy. His message is 'Think like them, live like them!'

Paul says this for one last time.
Philippians 4:8-9

(These two verses sum up the whole letter. In the final part of the letter, Paul thanks the believers for their gift; Philippians 4:10-23.)

Main point

Think about the right things. **Do** what God's word teaches.

Something to work on

Many Christians believe that it does not matter much what they **think** about. The important thing is what they **do**. They want people to see that they are good Christians.

This is wrong. Our thoughts and attitudes lead to our actions. Ask God to help you to show this to your listeners. Jesus came to change our minds and our hearts. He came to set us free from wrong thoughts. We can only truly live right when we have right thoughts first.

Notes

Philippians 4:8. Fill your minds with good things! Paul uses many different words to explain 'good things'. 'Noble' means valuable. 'Admirable' ('honourable') also means valuable, or attractive.

Philippians 4:9. Paul has taught them many things. He taught them when he was at Philippi. He taught them in this letter. They also know how Paul lives. He does what he teaches. Here Paul says 'You do it!' It is not enough to learn; we must **live** as Christians.

→ PREACH: Philippians 4:8-9

THINK RIGHT!
📖 *Philippians 4:8*

- What did Paul like to think about?
- What do you like to think about?
- How well does that fit with Philippians 4:8?

The way we think is very important. It makes us the people that we are. The more we think like Jesus, the more like Jesus we will be.

> *We can find it hard to fight wrong thoughts. Wrong thoughts about sex, or money. Jealous thoughts, angry thoughts, selfish thoughts. Bring them to God now and ask him to forgive you. Ask God to help you to listen to his word today. Ask him to help you to learn to think about good things.*

- How can Christians train their thoughts? [Discuss this together.]

Many things help us. We must control what we watch, what we read and what we hear. Ask 'Is it true and good?' We can help each other, as we talk about good things. We must not give up quickly. God's Spirit will help his people, but it takes a long time to change how we think. Pray about it every day.

The best way to control our thoughts is to **obey** Philippians 4:8! God tells us to think about **true, pure and lovely** things. If we fill our minds with good things, there will not be room for rubbish!

> *Here are some ideas. Find more. Think how you can help other people. Find out about Christians who suffer for Jesus, and pray for them. Write to missionaries. Think how you can tell other people about Jesus. Read books that will help you learn about God.*

The best thing to think about is **the Bible**. 📖 *Philippians 4:8.* The Bible is all those good things! Every day, read the Bible. Try to remember parts of it. Think about it at work, in the house, in the garden.
📖 *Psalm 19:7-11*

DO RIGHT!
📖 *Philippians 4:9*

Imagine the church at Philippi. They are very pleased to have this letter from Paul. They read it through together. The important part comes next! Will they put the letter away and forget about it? Or will they read it again, until they remember it? And will they **do** what God says to them through Paul?

> *What about you and me? We do not meet only to learn what the Bible says. We need to do it. Discuss how this letter has changed you so far. What things do you need to work on?*

STUDY: Philippians 4:10-13

19 HOW TO BE CONTENT

◉ Background

As Paul finishes his letter, he says thank you. His friends at Philippi sent him a gift in prison.

Paul does not only say thank you! He also has some more lessons. He wants us to learn more about how Christians think;
 📖 *Philippians 4:10-23*

◉ Main point

Christians can learn to be content in Jesus, whatever life is like.

✦ Something to work on

How to be content is important for many of us. ('Content' means that we are happy inside with what God has given us.) Too many Christians want to learn how to be rich, not how to be content!

This also speaks to people who are not Christians. Many people live unhappy lives. They always try to make things better. But even if they become rich, they are still not happy. Paul is content because he knows Jesus. Jesus satisfies all his desires. (Change the talk outline if your people are not Christians.)

◉ Notes

Philippians 4:10. The Christians at Philippi often helped Paul. They sent money to help him with the missionary work. (Philippians 4:15-16). They had not been able to do this for a long time. But Paul knew that they had not forgotten him. They did not have the chance to send help.

Philippians 4:11. Paul loved their gifts, but he was also happy without the gifts! He had learned to be happy when he had nothing!

Philippians 4:13. Jesus makes us content. It may seem impossible to be content, but all things are possible when we trust Jesus. Jesus' power makes us strong, as we trust him. (Paul does not mean that he can do anything that he wants to, through the power of Jesus. He means that he can go through anything that God sends him, through the power of Jesus.)

→ PREACH: Philippians 4:10-13

CONTENT INSIDE
📖 *Philippians 4:10-12*

Paul was so happy when Epaphroditus came with the gift from Philippi! But Paul was also happy **before** he came. Why?

- Think of all the reasons why Paul could have been unhappy. (He had no freedom, the chains were painful, he had been in prison for many months, he did not know what would happen to him…)

But Paul was content to wait in prison. Why? Because he was content **inside**. He did not need freedom to make him happy! He did not need comfort to make him happy! He did not need money to make him happy. Are you like that?

⊕ Imagine that you own a farm. You have all the food you need. You have your own well. You make your own power from a river. You do not need anything from outside. Everything comes from inside your own farm.

Paul was like that farm. He had everything he needed **inside** him. Whatever happened to him on the outside, he was still content.

❯❯ *Are you content inside? Or do you believe that a nice house will make you happy? Or more money? Or a better job? Or a husband or wife?*

❯❯ *But what do you find? When you get one thing, you want something else. You are still not satisfied! This is because you need to be content **inside**.*

You may think that life is too hard for you to be content. You have too much pain. Remember that Paul says 'I have **learned** to be content'. It was not easy. It can take many years. But God wants to teach us to be content.

So how is this possible? How **can** Christians be content **inside**?

CONTENT IN JESUS
📖 *Philippians 4:13*

⊕ Think of that farm. Everything comes from inside, but not from you! Jesus is our food and water and power. Jesus provides everything. That is how we can be content. It does not make life easy! But we trust Jesus to help us through. Believers **can** be content even when life is very hard. This is because our Father has planned these things and our Saviour gives us strength for them.

❯❯ 📖 *John 7:37-38. Do not try to be happy with **other** things! Jesus is the living water **inside** us. If you have Jesus, you may not have money or houses or health. But you will have forgiveness, peace and heaven. You will live with him for ever. So are you content?*

20 STUDY: Philippians 4:14-23
GIVING TO GOD

◉ Background
As Paul finishes his letter, he thanks his friends for their kind gift. And he tells them what God thinks of their generous attitude;
📖 *Philippians 4:14-23*

◉ Main point
Give to God—it is worship! Give to God—trust him to look after you!

◉ Something to work on
Never preach about giving because you want the church to give you more money! Paul did not want more gifts (Philippians 4:17). Trust God to look after your needs (Philippians 4:19).

How generous is your church? Do you give money to help other churches, or missionaries? Could the church give this week's money away? This could be the best way to worship God (Philippians 4:18).

◉ Notes
Philippians 4:15-16. Philippi was in the area called Macedonia. Most of these Christians were poor. Even so, they sent money to Paul. This helped him to tell about Jesus in other cities (2 Corinthians 8:1-5).

Philippians 4:17. Paul loves these Christians to give money. It will help **them**, not him! Paul uses a picture. It is as if God puts ('credits') their gifts to him into **their** bank account! Paul does not mean money. He means that when they give, God will **bless** them in many ways.

Philippians 4:18. The gifts to Paul are really worship to God! The gifts smell sweet ('fragrant') to God.

Philippians 4:19. It is as if God has a big house full of precious things for his people. Jesus got all this for believers when he died on the cross. So we never need to be worried. God will look after us!

Philippians 4:22. Caesar (Emperor in Rome) told the whole world to worship him. But some of his own servants worshipped Jesus! This gave Paul great joy.

Philippians 4:23 (Philippians 1:2). These are not just words to finish a letter with. Jesus' grace is everything that they need. Grace is the free gift that starts with forgiveness and ends in heaven.

➔ PREACH: Philippians 4:14-23

UNUSUAL GIVING
📖 *Philippians 4:14-16*

Most Christians give only a little money to God. Paul loves these Christians a lot because they give **themselves** to him. They are his partners. They love the gospel as Paul does. They help him to tell other people about Jesus. This is why Paul is so happy. Their gift is much more than money. **No other** church has cared like this one.

> ❯❯ *Be like the Philippian Christians. You may not be able to give very much. The important thing is **how** you give. Give your heart. Give your prayers. Share in the gospel.*

SAFE GIVING
📖 *Philippians 4:17-19*

⊕ A Christian friend comes to you with a gift. You know that she needs it herself. You are afraid that she will suffer. Perhaps you say 'Thank you, but I cannot take this from you'.

- Is this right? **Will** she suffer, if her gift comes from her love of Jesus?
  📖 *Philippians 4:17*

Paul did not worry about his friends! He was glad that they gave. It would be **good** for them, because God would bless them.

⊕ Now imagine that your friend has another good friend, who is very, very rich. Would you worry about her then? No, her rich friend will give her everything that she needs. 📖 *Philippians 4:19.*

[Talk a lot about this wonderful promise. How rich is God? How much does he care for his people? He has better things to give than money! What riches does God have for them 'in Christ'? What does Jesus' death promise believers? (Romans 8:32)]

> ❯❯ *Why do you find it hard to give your money? When you love Jesus, it is safe to give! He will look after you. He will give you better things than money!*

WORSHIP GIVING
📖 *Philippians 4:18, 20*

• What kind of worship pleases God?

Epaphroditus' long journey was like a long worship meeting, full of praise! This gift praised God more than songs do! It was like a sweet smell to God. Their love went up to God. And he was very pleased.

> ❯❯ *Be like the Philippian Christians. You may not be able to give very much. The important thing is how you give. Give your hearts. Give your prayers. Share in the gospel.*

E: LESSONS FROM PHILIPPIANS

It is important to take lessons from God's Word into our lives. It will help your people to discuss these questions in groups and pray about them. The questions help us to learn some of the main lessons from this letter. You can use these questions after you have finished all your talks on Philippians. Or you may want to use them after each chapter.

Philippians chapter 1

1. **Love for other believers**
   Philippians 1:3-5, 8, 24
   - 'Love for the same gospel glues Paul and the Philippian church together'? Do you find the same thing? How does this love show in your church and in your life?
   - How much does your love for other Christians cost you?

2. **Working together for Jesus**
   Philippians 1: 5, 18, 27
   - What makes it better to work together than on our own?
   - What makes it hard to work together?

3. **To live and die for Christ**
   Philippians 1:20-25
   - Do you wamt to be with Christ? Are you afraid of death?
   - Do you have a desire to live for Christ now? What choices will this mean?

4. **Lives that fit the gospel message**
   Philippians 1:27
   - What behaviour does not fit the gospel?
   - What behaviour makes people want to hear about Jesus?

Philippians chapter 2

1. **Like Jesus**
   Philippians 2:1-8
   - Discuss what makes it hard to be a servant.
   - What changes will help us to be more like Jesus?

2. **Like stars**
   Philippians 2:14-16
   - What you find difficult about the world we live in? What sins make it a 'dark' place?
   - So how can we 'shine as stars' when other people live in the dark?

3. **Like Timothy**
   Philippians 2:20-22
   - What do you like about Timothy? How can we be more like him?
   - Why did Paul trust Timothy so much? Do people trust you like this?

4. **Like Epaphroditus**
   Philippians 2:25-30
   - What do you like about Epaphroditus? What can you learn from him?
   - Epaphroditus was ready to put the gospel first, and even risk his life. Who do you know like that? Do you honour them? In what ways can you be more like them?

Philippians chapter 3

1. **The wrong kind of teachers**
   Philippians 3:2-3, 18-19
   - What kind of teaching and living show up false teachers?
   - What should we do when people like this teach in your town?

2. **Good works will not save you**
   Philippians 3:3-9
   - Did you once think that God was pleased with you because of what you did? How much were all Paul's good works worth?
   - How confident are you in Jesus? Are you sure that Jesus has done everything you need to make you right with God?

3. **Knowing Christ more and more**
   Philippians 3:10
   - So what things get in the way of us knowing Christ better? What great power does Paul pray for? How can this power help you to know Christ better?
   - When you suffer for Jesus, how does it help you to know him more?

4. **People who belong to heaven**
   Philippians 3:14, 20-21
   - Do you think of your life as a race towards heaven? How will this help you?
   - Do you want Jesus to come back soon? Why or why not?

Philippians chapter 4

1. **Rejoice in the Lord!**
   Philippians 4:4
   - Paul, in prison, shows so much joy in this letter. What stops your joy?
   - What things about Jesus give you joy? How can we help each other to have joy in Jesus?

2. **What to do with worry** *Philippians 4:6-7*
   - What do you worry about? How does it feel to worry?
   - Is it hard to do what God tells us here? What stops you from praying like this?

3. **Learning to be content** *Philippians 4:11-13*
   - Sometimes we may not be happy with what God has given us. Why is that?
   - How do we learn to be content? (Think why Paul was content.)

4. **Giving to God**
   Philippians 4:10, 14-19
   - Do you find it hard to give money and time to God? What makes it hard?
   - How does God feel when we give from our hearts?

F: TRAINING GUIDE:
how to preach Philippians

This training guide will help you learn how to prepare talks. (You can then use these steps for preparing talks from other parts of the Bible.)

Before you use this book, here are 5 studies to train you to prepare a talk. You can do these studies on your own. Or, if you can, meet as a group of preachers. Then you can help each other to learn. We encourage you to think of other men you can help to preach. This training guide will help you to help them. If you meet to study God's Word together, you will help each other. Then you will preach God's word more clearly.

Meet once a week for 5 weeks. Look at one study each time that you meet. You will work through these things:

- **The message of the letter**
- **how to get the background**
- **what the passage says**
- **how to find the main point**
- **how the passage speaks to us.**

This will mean that you understand the passage well. Then you will be able to prepare and preach clearly.

Remember how important it is to pray! Ask God to help you as you study His Word. How we need the help of the Holy Spirit as we think how to preach!

If you are meeting as a group, there is some work **before your first meeting**. You all need to read the letter to the Philippians and do some study questions (see the next pages).

STUDY 1. THE WHOLE LETTER

When you write a letter, you do not just put different thoughts down on the paper. Usually you have a reason to write. You think carefully how to explain what you want to say.

We need to think of Philippians as a real letter from Paul to Christians he knew in Philippi. He does not just write some nice thoughts! He knows what he wants to say. He writes very carefully. He wants to help these Christians. And Philippians is also God's letter to us today. So, as Paul writes to the Philippians, God speaks his words to them and to us.

Before your group study

Read Paul's letter a few times and think of these questions. (Do not use 'Preaching Philippians' to help you!)

1. Where is Paul? Who has visited him and why?

2. What can we learn about the Philippian Christians (see also Acts 16)?

3. Why does Paul write?

4. What are the main things Paul wants to say? Why does he want to say them?

5. Does Paul repeat any words or ideas?

At your group study

Discuss your answers to the 5 study questions.

Do you have some different answers?

Which ones help you to understand Paul's letter better?

You may have several answers to questions 3 and 4. Paul has more than one reason to write. He has a number of important things that he wants to say.

- That makes it hard to find a title or 'big idea' that tells us what the whole letter is about. One idea is 'gospel thinking'. This heading helps us to understand Paul's reasons for writing. Paul wants to train these believers to **think** rightly. He wants the **gospel** (the truth about Jesus) to change them.

(Example; in Philippians 1, Paul wants them to think rightly about him in prison. He wants them to have joy because the gospel is still spreading.)

Talk about this

Now read together the section in this book called 'about Paul's letter to the Philippians' (page 7).

- Does this agree with what you have found out?

- Is there anything new?
  Can you now see where it comes from?

As you study Philippians, this understanding of the whole letter will help you to understand the smaller sections. You can look at the smaller sections 'in context' (in their proper place in the whole letter).

Try to remember what you have learned.

STUDY 2. THE BACKGROUND

Look at the first picture of a plane. You understand what it is. Now look at second picture with the background. You understand a lot more –

- You see whether it is in the country or in the city – what does that tell you about the plane?

- You may see people round the plane – perhaps they are people that you know.

- If you can see the people coming out of the plane it may tell you why they travelled. It may be someone coming home – or a sick person coming to the hospital.

The background makes a big difference.

So when we study God's word, we try to see the background. Remind yourself what you have read from the whole letter. What did you learn about why Paul was writing? This is the background.

Try to understand the people in Philippi and what it was like for them. How did they feel? Imagine that you were there. This helps to understand the words in the section.

Example 1: Philippians 1:1-5

1. Think about Paul as he writes this letter.

- Where is he and why? (Philippians 1:13)
- Notice that Timothy was with him. Timothy also cared about the Philippian believers.
- When Paul thinks about the Philippian Christians, what does he feel? Why?
- Paul would like to visit these believers (**Philippians 2:19-24**). He cannot visit them now, so he writes to them. What does he want the letter to do for them (make them feel sad for him, encourage them, tell them off...?)
- What does Paul call himself and Timothy (Philippians 1:1)? What does this show?

2. Think about the Philippians as they receive this letter.

- Acts 16 tells us who some of these believers were.
- Remember that they sent a love gift to Paul in prison.
- How do you think they feel as they read Philippians 1:1-5?
- Does this section make them feel more love for Paul? Why?
- What is their 'partnership in the gospel'? Read on in Philippians 1 to find out what Paul means. How do Paul and the Philippians think the same about the gospel?

Example 2: Philippians 1:6-8

A lot of the background is the same as for Philippians 1:1-5. Remind yourself of this.

- As Paul thinks about these Christians in Philippians 1:6-8, what two things does he feel?
- Why does Paul think like this about the believers? What does he know about them? Why does this fill him with love and confidence?

- Why do you think Paul says that he feels confident about these Christians? Did they need encouraging?   **Philippians 1:27-30** shows that things were hard for them! Paul wants them to carry on as Christians.

STUDY 3. WHAT DOES IT SAY?

Look at the photo of the plane. Look carefully at the plane and the people. What can you learn? What is the reason for the flight?

In the same way, we must **look carefully** at what the Bible says. We must not think that we already know what it says! Here are some questions to ask –

1. **What exactly** does Paul say?

2. **Why** does he say it?

3. Is there anything unusual?

4. Is there anything that you do not understand?

5. Does he **repeat** any words or ideas?

Example 1: Philippians 1:1-5

Look carefully at what Paul says.

- **Ask the 5 questions.**

1. What exactly does Paul say?
2. Why does he say it?
3. Is there anything unusual?
4. Is there anything that you do not understand?
5. Does he repeat any words or ideas?

Then use the **STUDY** section on page 10 to help you.

Some things that you may have noticed:

- Often in his letters, Paul writes to the 'saints'. Here Paul also talks about 'overseers and deacons' (leaders).

- Philippians 1:3, 4 show special joy. What does this tell about Paul's friendship with these believers?

- 'Partnership in the gospel' (Philippians 1:5) is unusual. Paul does not write this to other churches. What does this tell about this church?

Example 2: Philippians 1:6-8

Ask the 5 questions and use the **STUDY** page to help you (page 12).

1. What exactly does Paul say?
2. Why does he say it?
3. Is there anything unusual?
4. Is there anything that you do not understand?
5. Does he repeat any words or ideas?

Some things that you may have noticed:

- Paul says that he is confident about these Christians. Then he gives some reasons. This shows that he really wants them to feel confident in God.

- Paul repeats (Philippians 1:7,8) how much he loves these believers (see also Philippians 1:3,4). Why does he say this so much?

STUDY 4. THE MAIN POINT

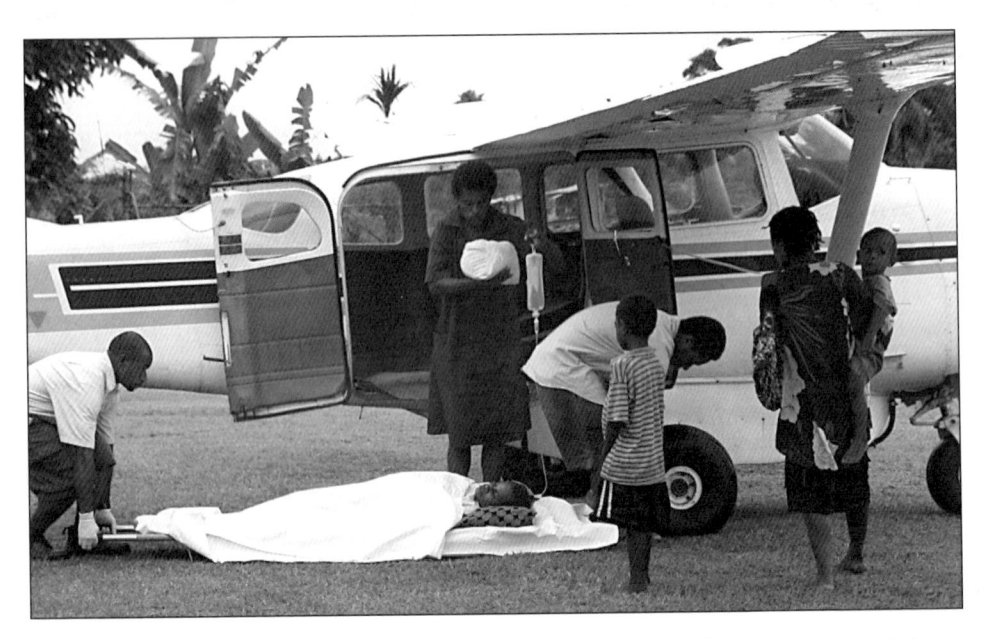

Imagine that you had to describe the photo of the plane. There are many things that you could say. You could make a long list like this—
- The plane was small with one engine
- It was white
- There were 6 people in it

Sometimes our talks are like that. We say many true things, but **they miss the point.**

See how the nurses carry a person out of the plane to the hospital. **That is the point of the photo!** It does not matter that the plane is small or white!

Always ask this question: **'what is the main point (big idea)?'**

Or, 'If Paul could only say one thing in the section, what would it be?'

We will say many things in our talk. Sometimes we will want to talk about details. **But we want everyone to go away with the main point in their minds.** We must make sure that we do not miss this.

Example 1: Philippians 1:1-5

You could talk about Paul's thankful prayers for these Christians. (But this is not the main point.) **Why** is Paul so thankful and full of joy? When he thinks of the Philippians, Paul thinks **'partners in the gospel'**. He praises God that this church thinks in the same way as he does. They want everyone to hear about Jesus, like he does. And they do everything they can to help in the gospel.

So the main point is this:

Paul and the Philippians Christians are partners. They help each other in the work of the gospel.

Now look at the **PREACH** page on Philippians 1:1-5 (page 11).

- Look at the headings. Do they help to make the main point? Do they help to explain the rest of the section, but not miss the main point?

Example 2: Philippians 1:6-8

Try to work out the main point of this passage.

Then look at **MAIN POINT** in the **STUDY** page on Philippians 1:6-8 (page 12).

- Do you agree with what we wrote? Does it say what Paul wants to say? Can you make it better?
- Do the headings on the PREACH page help to make the main point?

STUDY 5. HOW IT SPEAKS TO US

We can enjoy other people's photos. But when they are our photos of people that we know, the photos are much more interesting. Imagine that the person on the plane was your child! He was close to death because of a snake bite! Now the photo really speaks to you!

When you read Philippians, remember that—
- Paul writes to Christians in Philippi hundreds of years ago
- God writes to us today

As we understand what Paul says to the Christians then, **God** speaks his word to **us today**. This is because the Bible is God's living word. God's Spirit brings to life the words on the page.

When we teach God's word, we do not only want to teach *about* the Bible. We pray for God's words to speak *to us all*. We pray for God's words to change us.

Some study questions

- How does **the main point** speak to us today? How is it the **same** as for the Christians in Philippi? How is it **different**?

- Think of the **different people** that you will speak to. How does the main point speak to the children, people who are not yet believers, weak Christians…

- What **questions** will your listeners have? (What does this mean for me at home with the children? How is what you say true, when it does not seem to fit with real life?)

- **What else** in the Bible section is important for your listeners? Does it help them with weak areas? Does it help them with things that people find difficult? Does it warn them about dangers that Christians face?

Examples: Philippians 1:1-5 and Philippians 1:6-8

For both talks—

Use the study questions to think how to bring God's word home to your listeners.

Now think about the parts in the PREACH section which look LIKE THIS.

- *How do they help to bring the main point home to your listeners? What more do you need to say to make it clear?*

- *What other points do we make? Are these helpful?*

Remind yourself of all the things that you have learned as you studied the passage. Remember the main point and how that speaks to your listeners.

Remember to pray and ask for God's help

Now you are ready to write your talk in your own language. It is good to write it, because it helps you to be clear. Use the PREACH pages to help you. We give you the bones of the talk. You will need to put meat on the bones. You will need to explain things more and find more word pictures. Add in more about how the main point speaks to our lives.

We have taught you a way to study the rest of Philippians. For each section of Philippians, work through BACKGROUND, WHAT DOES IT SAY, MAIN POINT, HOW IT SPEAKS TO US.

Do your own study first and then look at "Preaching Philippians"!

If you have studied this in a group, it will help you to study the rest of Philippians together. We pray that this training guide will help you to prepare and preach Philippians better.

Preaching Philippians

© Phil Crowter/The Good Book Company 2009

Published by
The Good Book Company Ltd
Elm House, 37 Elm Road
New Malden, Surrey KT3 3HB, UK
email: ppp@thegoodbook.co.uk
UK: www.thegoodbook.co.uk
N America: www.thegoodbook.com
Australia: www.thegoodbook.com.au
New Zealand: www.thegoodbook.co.nz

Unless indicated, all Scripture references are taken from the HOLY BIBLE, NEW INTERNATIONAL VERSION. Copyright © 1973, 1978, 1984 International Bible Society. Used by permission.

ISBN: 9781906334925

Printed in China

| The *Pray Prepare Preach* project is working in partnership with a growing number of organisations worldwide, including: Langham Partnership Grace Baptist Mission Pastor Training International (PTI) Sovereign World Trust Africa Inland Mission (AIM) Worldshare Entrust Foundation India Bible Literature | African Pastors' Book Fund Preacher's Help African Christian Textbooks (ACTS) Nigeria Orphans for Christ, Uganda Project Timothy *Also in this series:* Preaching God's Big Picture Preaching Mark *Coming soon:* Preaching Job |